LONG KNIFE

The story of the fighting U. S. Cavalry
of the 1860 frontier

LONG

The story of the fighting U. S. Cavalry of the 1860 frontier

KNIFE

Written and Illustrated by Glen Dines

The Macmillan Company, New York, 1961

© Harry G. Dines 1961

Library of Congress catalog card number: 61-17256

First Printing

The Macmillan Company, New York

Brett-Macmillan Ltd., Galt, Ontario

Printed in the United States of America

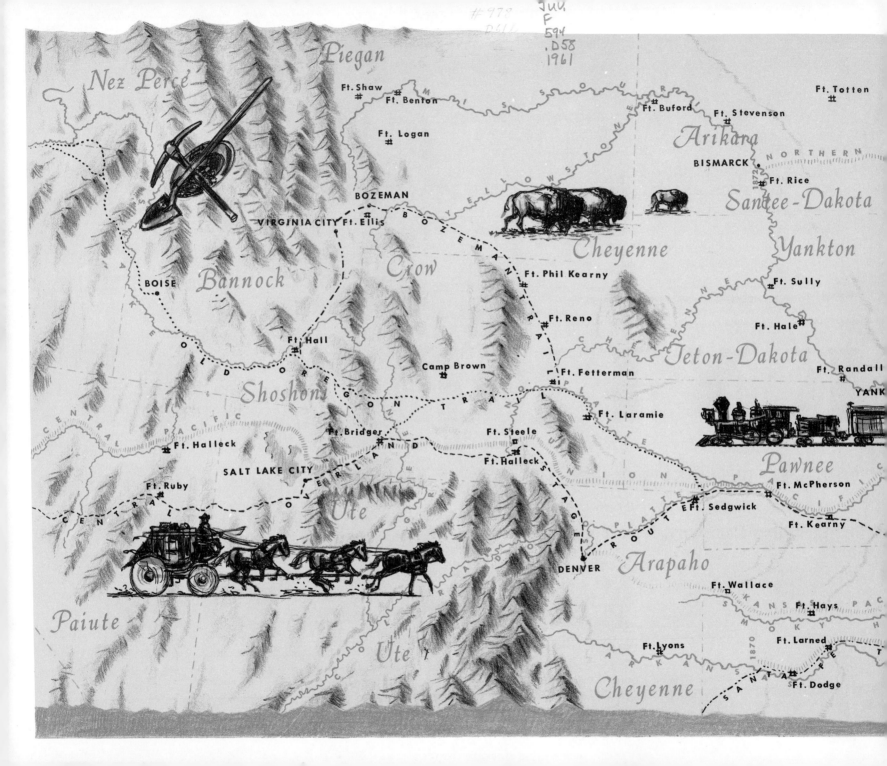

Nez Percé

Piegan

Ft. Shaw

Ft. Benton

Ft. Logan

Ft. Totten

Ft. Buford

Ft. Stevenson

Arikara

BISMARCK

Ft. Rice

Santee-Dakota

Yankton

BOZEMAN

VIRGINIA CITY Ft. Ellis

Bannock

Crow

Cheyenne

BOISE

Ft. Phil Kearny

Ft. Sully

Ft. Reno

Ft. Hale

Ft. Hall

Shoshoni

Camp Brown

Ft. Fetterman

Teton-Dakota

Ft. Randall

YANK

Ft. Laramie

Ft. Bridger

Ft. Halleck

Ft. Steele

Ft. Halleck

Pawnee

SALT LAKE CITY

Ft. Ruby

Ute

Ft. McPherson

Ft. Sedgwick

Ft. Kearny

DENVER

Arapaho

Paiute

Ute

Ft. Wallace

Ft. Hays

Ft. Lyons

Ft. Larned

Cheyenne

Ft. Dodge

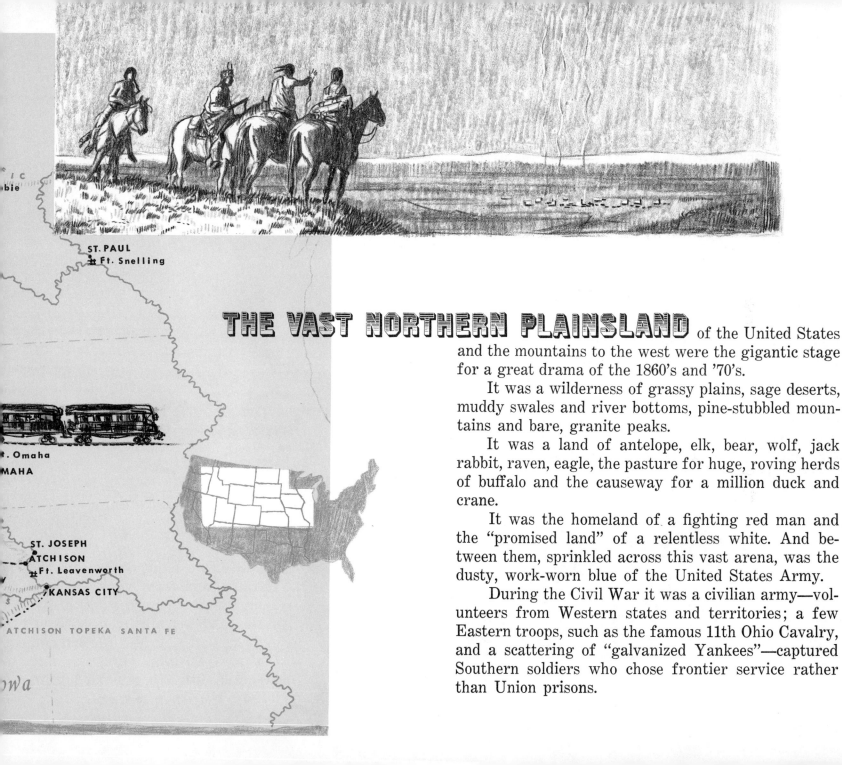

ST. PAUL
⚔ Ft. Snelling

. Omaha
MAHA

ST. JOSEPH
ATCHISON
⚔ Ft. Leavenworth

KANSAS CITY

ATCHISON TOPEKA SANTA FE

I C
bie

owa

THE VAST NORTHERN PLAINSLAND of the United States
and the mountains to the west were the gigantic stage
for a great drama of the 1860's and '70's.

It was a wilderness of grassy plains, sage deserts,
muddy swales and river bottoms, pine-stubbled mountains and bare, granite peaks.

It was a land of antelope, elk, bear, wolf, jack
rabbit, raven, eagle, the pasture for huge, roving herds
of buffalo and the causeway for a million duck and
crane.

It was the homeland of a fighting red man and
the "promised land" of a relentless white. And between them, sprinkled across this vast arena, was the
dusty, work-worn blue of the United States Army.

During the Civil War it was a civilian army—volunteers from Western states and territories; a few
Eastern troops, such as the famous 11th Ohio Cavalry,
and a scattering of "galvanized Yankees"—captured
Southern soldiers who chose frontier service rather
than Union prisons.

By 1866 the regular army was once again on the northern frontier—a tiny force of never more than fifteen thousand men faced with the staggering job of patrolling a million square miles of wilderness—one soldier for every fifty square miles!

The number of active military posts on the northern frontier grew from five in 1860 to more than thirty in 1868. However, many of these were tiny garrisons for one hundred or two hundred men, built beside a river "away out in the middle of nowhere" by clerks, cooks or cavalrymen of whatever was handy at the time: wood, stone or mud and sagebrush—lonely, little islands of buildings in the midst of a vast sea of scrub grass and sage or clustered at the foot of a mountain.

Many of the older forts, and some built in the '60's, were walled with stout palisades and bastions of 12-inch logs butted four feet into the earth. However, Indians rarely, if ever, attacked any fort and most outposts built after the late '60's were unprotected. And many so-called "forts," like the tiny guard posts strung along the overland telegraph line, were nothing more than a few sheds and crude stockades guarded by ten to fifteen men.

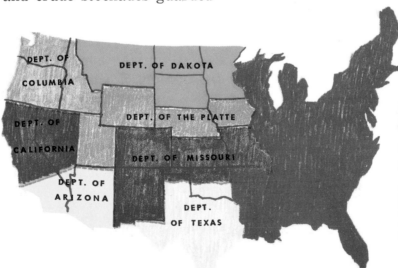

(Right) Departments of the Army around 1870. Each department had its own headquarters.

By 1870, the 1st, 3rd and 8th U.S. Cavalry regiments were on duty along the Pacific coast and in the states and territories of Nevada, Arizona and New Mexico; 2nd and 5th in Nebraska, Wyoming and Montana; 4th, 6th, 9th and 10th in Texas; the 7th in Kansas.

(Above) "Typical" outpost of late '60's. "Old" fort outlined in red dashes with bastion (block house) used as storeroom (11).

Commanding Officer's Quarters (1) and Officers' Quarters (2) usually on north edge of Parade Grounds opposite Company Barracks (4). Other buildings include: (3) Officers' dining and kitchen; (5) Company dining and kitchen; (6) "Suds Row"—for laundresses and married enlisted men; (7) Post adjutant; (8) Hospital; (9) Guardhouse; (10) Wainwright; (12) Powder magazine; (13) Harness maker; (14) Bakery—supplied out of funds saved by enlisted men; (15) Commissary; (16-17) Quartermaster storehouse and office; (18) Stables and corral; (19) Granery; (20) Saddler; (21) Blacksmith; (22) Post garden; (23) Icehouse; (24) Sutler's store; and (25) Cemetery.

At best, most of the buildings were cramped and crowded—stiflingly hot in summer, damp and cold in winter.

The food was drab and sometimes scanty. A month's menu might have included salt pork or beef, dried fish, beans, rice, dried vegetables, soft bread (if the post had a bakery) or hardtack, vinegar, molasses and the ever-present "Rio" coffee, brewed strong enough to "grow whiskers on a cannon ball."

The pleasures were few. A tiny sutler's store was

The buildings themselves were described as "cozy" by some, "hovels" or "mud huts" by others. They varied from Fort Laramie's big two-story barracks with shingled roofs and pane glass windows to long, narrow claptraps thrown together over raw dirt and plastered or chinked with mud that fell out in great gobs during cold weather.

often the only "social center" for three hundred men. Nearly all recreation was "home grown"—horse races, hunting or variety shows staged and performed by the soldiers. The few yearly holidays were celebrated with games of "Catch the Greased Pig," sack races and banquets of such delicacies as fresh strawberries, lemons or canned oysters ordered all the way from St. Joseph or Salt Lake City. If there were women on the post there might have been an occasional dance or picnic.

(Above) Company barracks of log with ventilator (A), rough-hewn lumber floor and stone foundation. Dirt roof (B) spread of layer of sticks and straw on pole rafters. "Cutaway" view includes: shelves (C) for haversacks, caps and clothing; bunk beds (D) often handmade by men and marked with name and Company letter; and gun rack (E). With straw for bedding and only one blanket issued during first two years of duty, two or three men sometimes slept together in cold weather. Buildings were lit by candles and heated with fireplaces or huge iron stoves.

The "old army" was a strange mixture of Minnesota farm boys and New Jersey clerks, toughs and drunkards, teachers and lawyers. There were "snowbirds" who enlisted in the fall and deserted in the spring and tough old "regulars" with service stripes from cuff to elbow. A huge post-Civil War immigration brought many foreign-born into the service— good soldiers like Saddler Julius Stickoffer, Company L, 8th Cavalry, who came from Switzerland to earn a Congressional Medal of Honor near Cienega Springs in Utah, or Irish-born Sgt. John H. Foley, who was awarded this great honor in action on the Platte.

The guardhouse was not unfamiliar to this tough, pipe-smoking, free-swinging lot who had little to do with officers or their enlisted men servants, called "dog robbers." Still, as a group, they were proud, well disciplined and splendid in the field.

Uniforms for cavalry in '60's and early '70's: Sergeant-Major (right foreground) in full dress with plumed hat, metal shoulder scales on jacket, saber, belt and sash; officer in frock coat and campaign hat; First Sergeant (facing troops), corporal and soldiers in ranks in "fatigue" or work clothes of sack coats and forage caps. Soldier without coat wears issued shirt but "nonregulation" suspenders. Other clothing issued enlisted men included hats, canvas stable frocks and "rubberized" ponchos.

(Left) Soldier in cavalry greatcoat with wrist-length cape. (Right) Plumed helmet, full dress for cavalry after 1872.

The base pay was $16 a month (reduced to $13 in 1872) with small increases after the third year and "bounties" for reenlistments made on the frontier—$34 at or near Ft. Kearney on the Platte to $142 in Washington Territory. This was small reward, however, for harsh and dangerous frontier duty with long, dreary hours of monotonous army routine and back-breaking labor.

And bedbugs, beans and iron-tipped arrows knew no rank. A gray-haired first lieutenant, commander of some forlorn, undermanned outpost, twice decorated veteran of the Civil War, missing three fingers from his left hand, could look forward to a captaincy after perhaps twenty years. In the meanwhile he would serve, sweat and fight for a meagre $125 a month; out of which he fed, clothed and raised his family and bought his own uniforms, side arms, saber, horses and saddles. But even then he might call himself lucky, for his "shavetail" adjutant might have been a Civil War captain, his first sergeant a colonel in the Volunteers and his chief bugler a West Point trained, ex-major of the Confederacy.

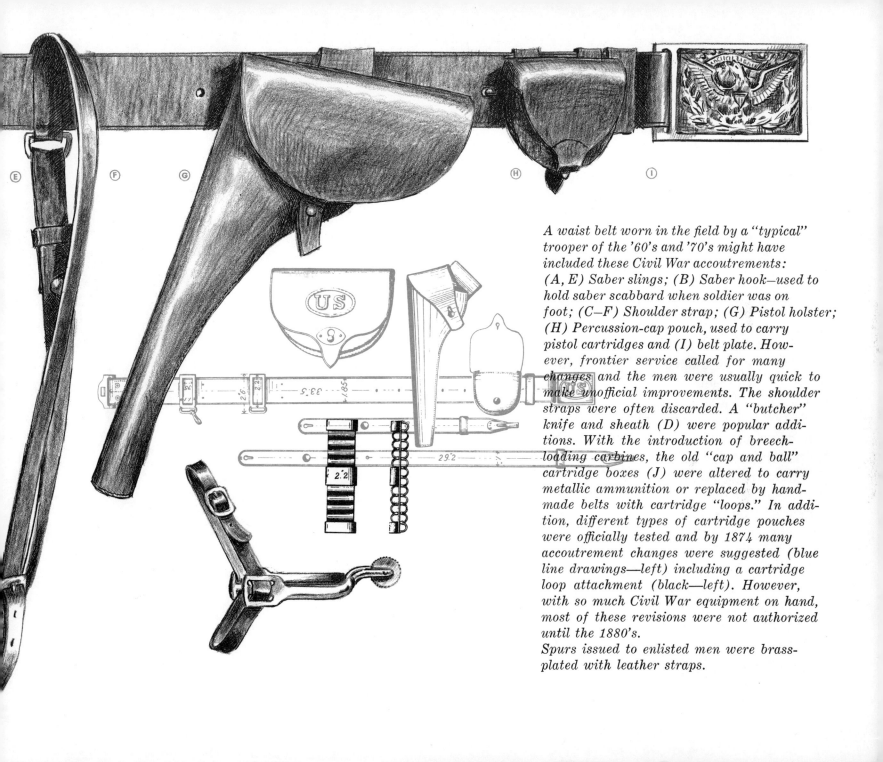

E   F   G   H   I

A waist belt worn in the field by a "typical" trooper of the '60's and '70's might have included these Civil War accoutrements: (A, E) Saber slings; (B) Saber hook—used to hold saber scabbard when soldier was on foot; (C–F) Shoulder strap; (G) Pistol holster; (H) Percussion-cap pouch, used to carry pistol cartridges and (I) belt plate. However, frontier service called for many changes and the men were usually quick to make unofficial improvements. The shoulder straps were often discarded. A "butcher" knife and sheath (D) were popular additions. With the introduction of breech-loading carbines, the old "cap and ball" cartridge boxes (J) were altered to carry metallic ammunition or replaced by hand-made belts with cartridge "loops." In addition, different types of cartridge pouches were officially tested and by 1874 many accoutrement changes were suggested (blue line drawings—left) including a cartridge loop attachment (black—left). However, with so much Civil War equipment on hand, most of these revisions were not authorized until the 1880's.

Spurs issued to enlisted men were brass-plated with leather straps.

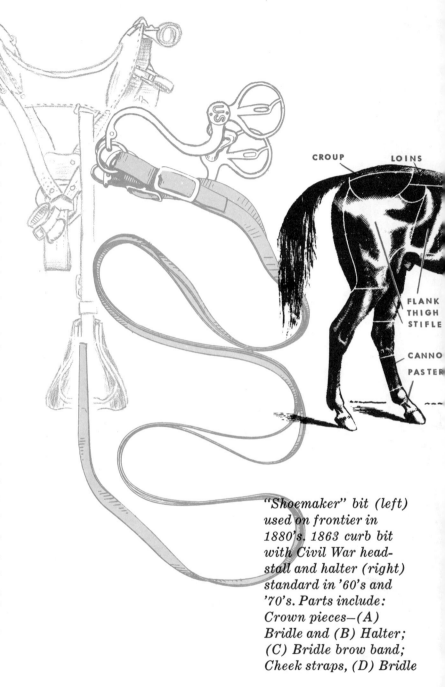

(Right) "Stripped" frontier model of Civil War McClellen saddle. Beechwood pommel and cantle and poplar seat covered with rawhide.

All the branches of the army served on the frontier, from the plodding "walk-a-heap" infantry to the struggling "wagon-gun" artillery. But the land was big and many of the jobs, like protecting more than five thousand miles of telegraph line, mail and stage route, wagon roads and rivers from a swift and cunning enemy, called for mounted troops. So it was that the "baby" of the family, the faster moving "long knife" cavalry, often saw more than its share of hard and dangerous duty.

Born of a marriage of the old Dragoons and Mounted Riflemen, the U.S. Cavalry was just four years old and six regiments strong at the close of the Civil War. A year later the valiant 7th, 8th, 9th and 10th regiments were added, the last two made up of Negro troops—the famous "Buffalo Soldiers."

Recruiting standards for all branches were much the same: age eighteen to thirty-five, able-bodied, good character; but the cavalry requirements of 1874 favored the lean, wiry type, with its selection limited to men between 5′5″ and 5′10″ in height and not over 150 pounds in weight. Horsemanship, however, was not mentioned. And, as often as not, the duties of a cavalryman had little to do with riding a horse. Making roads, building bridges, cutting wood, sawing ice or hours of dreary guard duty accounted for much of a trooper's time. And when he was in the saddle it was often as escort for a plodding, ox-drawn "bull wagon," or a slow-moving immigrant train.

CROUP   LOINS

FLANK
THIGH
STIFLE

CANNO
PASTER

"Shoemaker" bit (left) used on frontier in 1880's. 1863 curb bit with Civil War headstall and halter (right) standard in '60's and '70's. Parts include: Crown pieces—(A) Bridle and (B) Halter; (C) Bridle brow band; Cheek straps, (D) Bridle

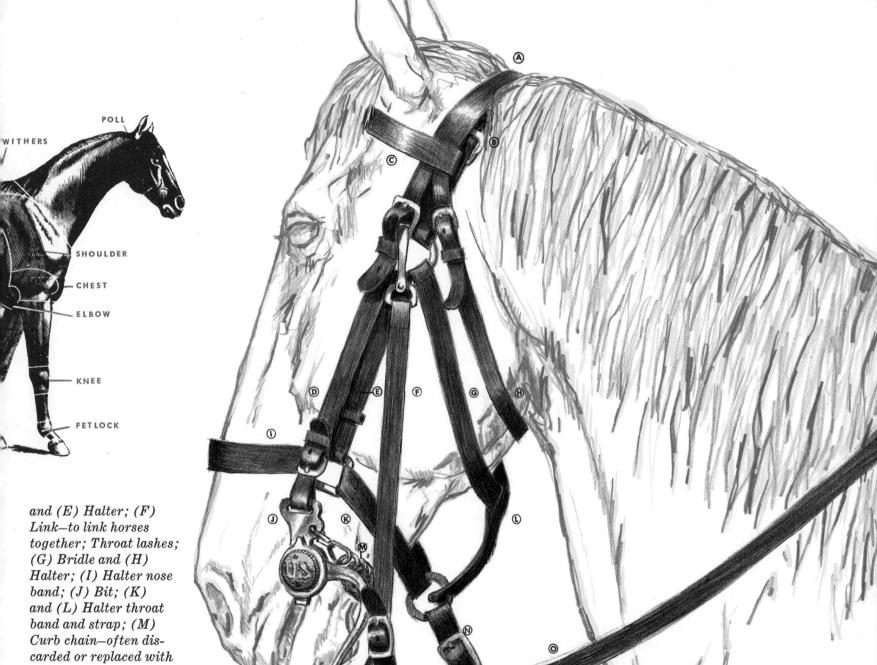

WITHERS

POLL

SHOULDER

CHEST

ELBOW

KNEE

FETLOCK

and (E) Halter; (F) Link—to link horses together; Throat lashes; (G) Bridle and (H) Halter; (I) Halter nose band; (J) Bit; (K) and (L) Halter throat band and strap; (M) Curb chain—often discarded or replaced with lighter strap; (N) Halter strap; (O) Reins.

But when the stage was set for fast action the cavalry was ready—from the fuzzy-cheeked recruit to the somber, bearded generals, Sheridan, Crook, Mackenzie, Cooke, Miles, Terry or the dashing, ill-fated Custer, or the colonels and captains, sergeants and corporals who rode and sweated and fought and died in a cruel, puzzling "war" that was often as unpopular as it was deadly.

And perhaps the best description of this drama can be found in the diaries of the men who lived it— the brief, scribbled notes of daily pleasure and pain, danger and delight that take us back to those times.

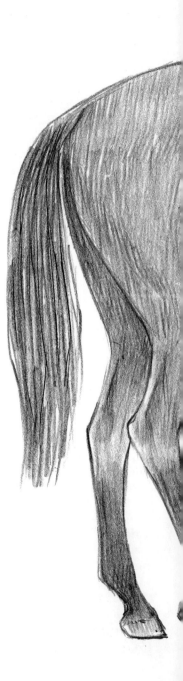

"May 20—No drill today. Cut wood all afternoon. 'Celebrated' at sutlers tonight. One year at fort. B., Charlie and self had splendid feed of canned peaches. Rumors of Indian troubles above Sage Creek. Sgt. Heimmer thinks we're in for 'little ride' tomorrow."

(Above) Drawing of regulation horse equipment in 1862 Ordnance Manual.

McClellen saddle, packed for field duty in '60's and '70's, (right) included: (A) Blanket roll with shelter tent, drawers, socks; (B) Saddle bags with ammunition, horseshoes, curry-comb, brush, tobacco, personal items; (C) Overcoat; (D) Forage sack with oats or corn; (E) Camp kettle—other men carried coffeepots, frying pans, etc.; (F) Haversack with hardtack, bacon, coffee, etc.; (G) Carbine socket; (H) Picket pin and lariat; (I) Canteen and cup; (J) "D" ring; (K) Girth. Total weight—70 to 100 pounds. Men wore jackets or sack coats and reenforced trousers but preferred forage caps or "store bought" wide-brim hats to campaign hats which lost shape quickly. Checked civilian "hickory" shirts were popular. Gauntlets not issued until '80's so few enlisted men could afford them in '60's and '70's.

"May 21—Heimmer right. 'Boots and Saddles' after breakfast. Co. C and det. of Co. A (Charlie, B., boy from Wisconsin, myself and 5 others) issued three day's rations. My hardtack mouldy. On road by 6. . . ."

At the first notes of "Assembly" for a mounted patrol many a wise old regular took his place with spare tobacco, extra sugar and coffee cadged from the mess hall, and a handmade bag slung over his saddle filled with parched corn for his horse. And as the column moved out he knew well the gritty taste of dust, the sharp stench of horse sweat and the age-old sounds of the cavalry—the snorts and whinnies, rattles and jangles, the yakkity-babble of the men, the squeak and squeeze of leather and the endless thumping scuff and clump of hooves.

". . . came upon stage station about 1:00. Stock-tender killed and scalped . . . poor man! Two others hid in nearby willows, both wounded. Building all burnt. Horses gone. Det. of Co. B escorting supply wagon came in with guide. Heard him say it was work of Cheyenne—part of big

band that crossed road further up. After burial we left main road to follow trail of savages."

Except for the main roads and rivers and a few miles between, the vast frontier was unmapped and largely unknown and the wanderings of the Indians an even greater puzzle. It was next to impossible for the army to carry the fight to the enemy without the help of civilian guides, like famous Jim Bridger, Kit Carson, "California" Joe and the host of other trappers, traders, mountain men and halfbreeds who knew the land and the ways of the Indians. And even then many a battle was won because the Indian scouts,

hired to help the guide in the tricky work of tracking a band of "hostiles" or locating their village, often joined in the attack as well. But since the Plains Indian tribes had been feuding among themselves long before the white man came and since nearly all Plains Indian men, hostile or friendly, were warriors at birth, to be offered a fine, blue coat, much food and one hundred dollars to track down and fight an age-old enemy was considered a rare bargain indeed for many an Osage, Arikara, Shoshoni or Crow. And some Indians even went so far as to join the white man's army, like the battalion of Pawnee recruited to protect the railroad construction crews along the Platte and led by the famous North brothers.

(Right) Coming-
Around-with-the-
Herd and Blue Hawk,
Pawnee scouts. Army
coat studded with
brass decorations.

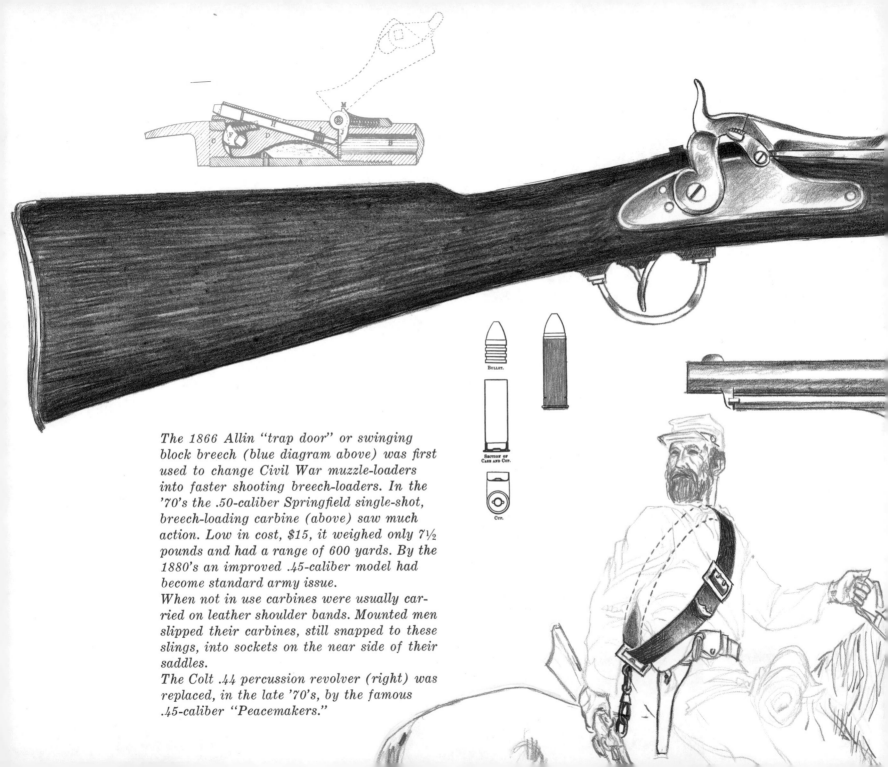

BULLET.

SECTION OF CASE AND CUP.

CUP.

The 1866 Allin "trap door" or swinging block breech (blue diagram above) was first used to change Civil War muzzle-loaders into faster shooting breech-loaders. In the '70's the .50-caliber Springfield single-shot, breech-loading carbine (above) saw much action. Low in cost, $15, it weighed only 7½ pounds and had a range of 600 yards. By the 1880's an improved .45-caliber model had become standard army issue.

When not in use carbines were usually carried on leather shoulder bands. Mounted men slipped their carbines, still snapped to these slings, into sockets on the near side of their saddles.

The Colt .44 percussion revolver (right) was replaced, in the late '70's, by the famous .45-caliber "Peacemakers."

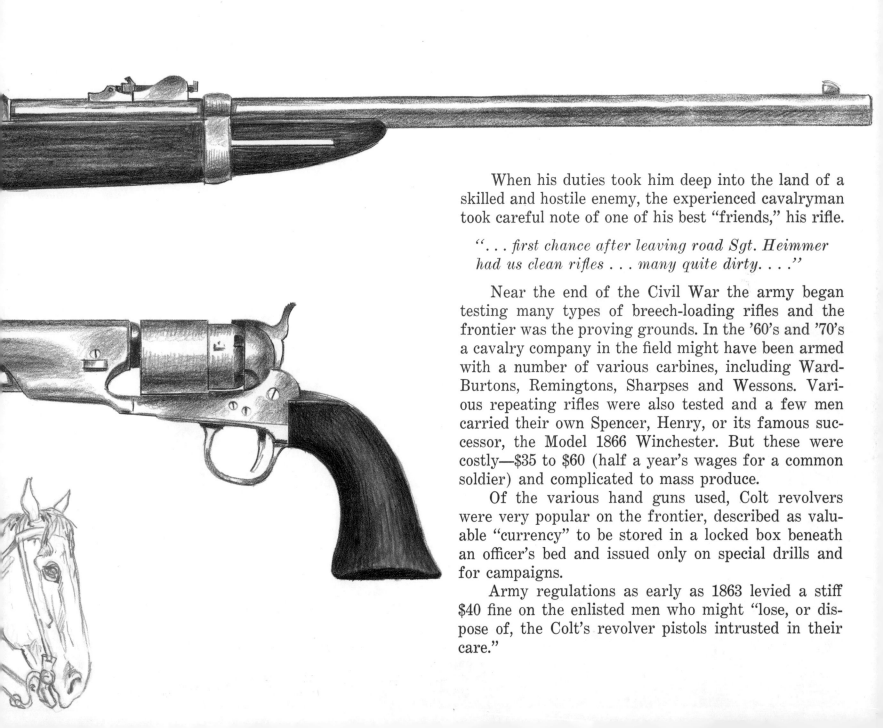

When his duties took him deep into the land of a skilled and hostile enemy, the experienced cavalryman took careful note of one of his best "friends," his rifle.

". . . first chance after leaving road Sgt. Heimmer had us clean rifles . . . many quite dirty. . . ."

Near the end of the Civil War the army began testing many types of breech-loading rifles and the frontier was the proving grounds. In the '60's and '70's a cavalry company in the field might have been armed with a number of various carbines, including Ward-Burtons, Remingtons, Sharpses and Wessons. Various repeating rifles were also tested and a few men carried their own Spencer, Henry, or its famous successor, the Model 1866 Winchester. But these were costly—$35 to $60 (half a year's wages for a common soldier) and complicated to mass produce.

Of the various hand guns used, Colt revolvers were very popular on the frontier, described as valuable "currency" to be stored in a locked box beneath an officer's bed and issued only on special drills and for campaigns.

Army regulations as early as 1863 levied a stiff $40 fine on the enlisted men who might "lose, or dispose of, the Colt's revolver pistols intrusted in their care."

SCOUTS   MAIN COMMAND

                                    GUIDON
                        CAPT.   — ꞋꞋ —   ≣ ≣ ≣ ≣ ≣ ≣꞊Ꞌ—≣ ≣ ≣
      —   BUGLER   CPL.   CPL. SGT.   CPL.

But when a cavalry column jogged loosely across a hostile land, even the best armed soldier was a target and every horse and mule a prize. So each man kept his place in the formation, from the scouts and advance guard to the flankers fanned far out on either side and the ever watchful rear guard.

". . . crossed a big alkali flat . . . all sage and dust. Sun very hot."

A tough, hard-riding cavalry outfit could make forty miles a day if need be, but usually the lay of the land, the location of fording places or the distance between water holes decided the length of a day's march. And in a hard, rawhide saddle with the sun a hot flat disk in a cloudless sky and dust and sweat searing skin, eyes and lips of horse and rider alike, fifteen miles could seem like a hundred.

CAPTAIN

1st LIEUTENANT

LIEUTENANT

SERGEANT MAJOR

Q.M. SERGEANT

1st SERGEANT

ORDNANCE SERGEANT

SERGEANT

CORPORAL

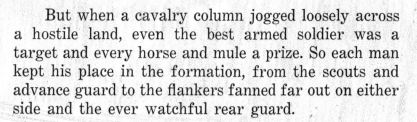

ESCORT

REAR GUARD

CPL.   LT.

1st SGT.

1st LT.   SGT.

(Left) Design of guidon used until 1863, then brought back in the late 1880's.

Near the end of a long day's march many soldiers would walk beside their tired mounts, stooping now and then to gather buffalo chips or twigs for the cook fire, or a wild onion to spice their meal. A few marksmen might be allowed to skirt the flanks in search of fresh meat for the camp kettles.

Once the campsite was selected and marked with the guidon there was a great bustle of activity, especially if it was a large regimental-size formation. Tents were set up, usually in two rows to form a "company street," with the officers' tents and a barricade of wagons at either end and the horses picketed in the middle, the wagons unloaded, sinks and fire pits dug, forage and grain set out, wood or chips gathered and the cook fires set ablaze.

With a smaller, faster-moving formation the troops might bivouac without tents, their only shelter a tiny lean-to of brush and branches set up beside the campfire, and this if there were trees nearby.

Yet in the middle of a trackless plain beside some nameless stream, the age-old army routine was followed to the sound of a strident bugle: Assembly, Guard Mount, Mess, Retreat or the soft poetry of "Taps" echoing across a vast and savage land—"Fades the light/ and afar/goes the day/and the stars/shineth bright/Fare thee well/day has gone/night is on."

Stable Call

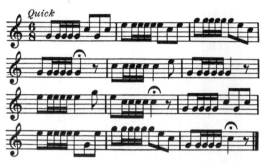

"Come all who are able and go to the stable,
Want water your horses and give 'em some corn,
For if you don't do it, the Cap'n will know it,
And then you will rue it, as sure as you're born.
So come to the stable, all ye who are able and
Water your horses and give 'em some corn."

To Horse

"Go to the picket line and get your horse,
You are to get him where 'er he may be of course."

Boots and Saddles

"Go to your horses
Bridle and saddle them up
Surcingles cinchas on them all."

Mess Call

"Soupy, soupy, soupy, without a single bean,
Coffee, coffee, coffee, without a bit of cream,
Porky, porky, porky, without a streak of lean."

(Left) 14" picket pin of 1860-1870. (Above) Swivel-top Lyon's used in '80's.

Long before "Taps," however, the men had seen to their tired horses—removing bridles and saddles and letting them roll, "cooling" them with blankets still on and then watering and feeding. In the winter the men often scraped away large areas of snow for grazing or stripped the bark from nearby cottonwoods for extra forage. Grooming by hand rub or currycomb and brush and careful inspection of ears, eyes, nose and hooves were very important. Most officers saw to it that a lazy soldier took good care of his horse, if nothing else.

But even with the finest care, many a Missouri-born, grain-fed gelding was no match for grueling cavalry service. During a long, hard campaign a single regiment sometimes lost as many as six hundred animals to starvation, hoof rot, pneumonia, heat stroke or sheer exhaustion.

Chunky, western-bred horses were best for frontier work where breed and speed were second to muscle and stamina. Indian villages were sometimes attacked more for their tough little ponies than anything else.

For their part, the Indians prized the big army mounts, not for work but for war and hunting. Many a new day on the frontier was announced by a galloping, robe-waving band of braves thundering down on a camp in an attempt to stampede the horses, while the soldiers rushed for their rifles and the bugler sounded "Stable" or "Water" to check any runaways.

"May 22—Indians charged the camp this morning. Scared off three horses, one of Lt. H.'s among them. He says with 10 men he would chase the cowards all way to Canada. Guide in from scouting about 10. Says Indians camped to east. B., Charlie, myself and others of Co. A escorted wagon while Capt. took others to strike Indian village. . . ."

Tough working ponies were not the only advantage enjoyed by the Indian. He knew the land and could travel fast. With a spare horse, his weapons and a handful of dried buffalo meat or pemmican an Indian could cover sixty miles a day for a week running.

But the Indian was also a skillful warrior and an excellent horseman and these qualities were often tragically underestimated. Of the three annihilations suffered by American armed forces, two came at the hands of the fierce Plains Indian—the Fetterman disaster in 1866 and the Custer debacle ten years later—and both were the kind of short, savage, hand-to-hand battles most preferred by the Indian, for whom the act of "counting coup"—touching an armed enemy with bare hand, stick or weapon—often brought greater honor than actually killing. And yet, while the Indian

was capable of this kind of reckless courage, he was also a deadly practical fighter who usually chose the kind of attack that seemed most likely to bring success for himself and his group—whether a bold frontal assault or the cunning ruse of sending out decoys to lure an unsuspecting enemy to disaster.

". . . soon after the others left we sighted three redskins riding nearby—one mounted on Lt. H.'s horse. We immediately took after them. . . ."

From 1866 to 1875 some four hundred engagements between Indian and cavalry were officially listed and probably as many more were not recorded. Most of these were deadly little fights of less than a hundred men that flared up throughout the vast frontier from Frenchman Creek in Nebraska, where Lt. Price led Company A of the 5th Cavalry in May, 1869, to a skirmish reported a few month's later by Lt. Stambaugh, Company D, 2nd Cavalry on the Popo Agie in Wyoming Territory some five hundred miles to the west.

"... hadn't gone 100 yards before whole passel of Indians came out of the ravine on both sides and right down our throats. Most of us managed to fall back to wagon but those in front cut off. Charlie among them. Doesn't know how he got back to wagon alive. Says boy from Wisconsin fell off his horse in excitement and he tried to help but Indians everywhere. Says if these are 'cowards' Lt. H. is going to chase to Canada, he'll wish him good luck. . . . We dismounted at wagon and formed skirmish line. Boys fought bravely and split the charge. Then Indians commenced to circle the wagon, bobbing and weaving. I fired as fast as I knew how. B. got arrow in his leg. A boy next to me was hit by ball but it was spent and didn't even break the skin . . . seemed an awful long time before we heard the main command coming back. . . ."

PISTOL ATTACK
⑥ GALLOP, HOOO

DRAW PISTOLS
⑤ TROT, HOOO

④ FRONT INTO FORAGERS, FORWARD, HOOO

① ATTENTION

COLUMN OF TWOS

③ COLUMN RIGHT, HOOO

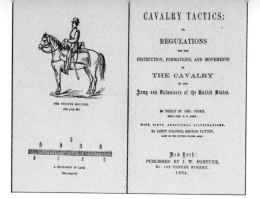

CAVALRY TACTICS:
OR,
REGULATIONS
FOR THE
INSTRUCTION, FORMATIONS, AND MOVEMENTS
OF
THE CAVALRY
OF THE
Army and Volunteers of the United States.

By PHILIP ST. GEO. COOKE,
BRIG.-GEN. U.S. ARMY.

WITH SIXTY ADDITIONAL ILLUSTRATIONS,
By LIEUT.-COLONEL GEORGE PATTEN,
LATE OF THE UNITED STATES ARMY.

New York:
PUBLISHED BY J. W. FORTUNE,
No. 102 CENTRE STREET.
1864.

(Left) Title page of Philip St. George Cooke's tactics manual used on frontier after 1864.

In a "war" of widely scattered, hit-and-run attacks, the cavalry struggled with tactics meant for moving large formations over short distances. But even then the demands of frontier duty left little time for drill, the backbone of battle training, while target practice was often limited to twelve rounds a year. And often a recruit learned to ride in the first miserable, skin-raw, bone-bruised weeks of a hard, month-long march.

Still the men learned. By the early '70's the heavy, unwieldy sabers were seldom seen on patrols or campaigns. By this time, also, the cavalry was probably fighting more on foot than horseback, since a skirmish line of dismounted troops firing carefully could often discourage a much larger force of mounted Indians. And in many fights, the actual firing was done by a few cool-headed marksmen with the other soldiers passing loaded carbines into their hands.

However, the frontier cavalry never lacked that one necessary thing that can never be taught—plain guts. It was this kind of valor that sent a handful of men through a curtain of whistling lead and arrows—and back again—to bring water to Reno's beleaguered command on the Little Big Horn, the spirit that brought the calm of courage to a ragged little company of cavalry, face to face with twice their number

CHARGE

of dangerous and cunning foes, and sent them fanning out over rock and sage, spurring their snorting mounts into a trot, then gallop and finally, with pistols raised and guidon fluttering against a flat blue sky, drove them forward in a headlong charge that filled the air with dust and the thunder of hooves and a wild, throaty chorus that echoed the bugle's brassy tune.

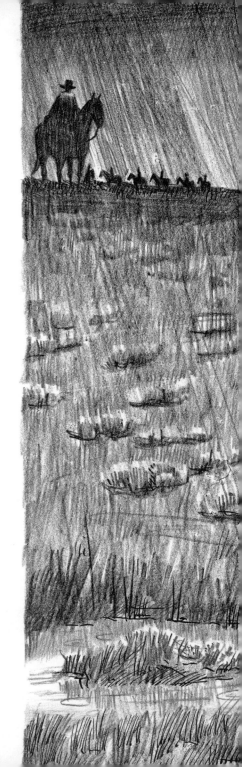

*"Jerk line" for 6-mule team (left)
was leather strap split at end to fasten
on both sides of near leader's bit.*

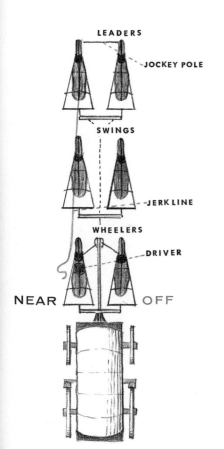

LEADERS

JOCKEY POLE

SWINGS

JERK LINE

WHEELERS

DRIVER

NEAR   OFF

*"May 23—Buried the Wisconsin boy in dark so
Indians can't find grave. Rain. Very cold. Wet
blankets and wetter clothes."*

"May 24—Rain. B.'s leg swelling bad.

*"May 25—Rain all morning. Indian trail washed
out. Turned back about noon. B.'s leg worse. Made
kind of Indian sled to carry him. Seven horses
gave out today. Rations low."*

Few prisoners were taken by either side and many
soldiers kept a spare cartridge for a quick and merciful
death as a last resort.

Even a slight wound could prove fatal. Only the
simplest medical aid could be given in the field, and the
hospitals in frontier outposts were usually undermanned and poorly equipped.

But the deadliest threat of all was the heat and
lung-clogging dust or the months of cold and wet of
the frontier itself. Flimsy, poorly ventilated barracks
or thin tents and soggy blankets were no match for
this harsh land. Year by year, sickness and disease
claimed two and three times as many men as the fierce
Cheyenne or Kiowa. Tuberculosis, pneumonia and
"flux"—diarrhea and dysentery—often struck down
whole companies. While typhoid, malaria and smallpox
ravaged Indian and white man alike.

The Indian Campaign Medal was authorized in 1905.

The total casualties of this struggle, compared to the total number of troops involved, were probably greater than the Civil War—called one of the deadliest conflicts in U.S. history.

"May 26—Reached the fort late afternoon. One boy died as we marched in. B. may lose his leg. Letters from home. They think Indian trouble about over because so little reports in newspapers. Sgt. H. just came in. Am on escort duty tomorrow. Wagon train to Rock Creek. Some immigrants killed there yesterday. Am very tired."

And so it was when the cavalryman toiled and fought on the plains and prairies and in the rugged mountains—from the bloody 1862 Sioux uprising in Minnesota, through the '60's and '70's and into the '80's when the wily Apache raided from his desert fastness and the valiant Sioux made his tragic "last stand" on a snow-covered battlefield in South Dakota. The last official campaign was in 1898 but as late as 1911 the rugged mountains of Nevada echoed the thunder of cavalry hooves when the army was called out to quell a ragged band of rebellious Paiute.

*(Above) Deadly Gatling gun—
1867 model. (Below) Sitting Bull,
famous Sioux Indian leader, photo-
graphed at Fort Randall in 1882
after his surrender.*

It was a cruel, total war with deeds of unmatched valor and unspeakable savagery on both sides—of great victories and crushing defeats—but the final outcome was never in doubt. In the huge panorama of history, a powerful, steel-age nation was stretching itself from sea to sea and for a brief moment the stalwart cavalry rode in the fore to brush aside a few stubborn bands of stone-age warriors.

The beginning of the end came when the first buffalo—the Plains Indians' main food supply—fell to a white man's gun and the first section of rich, black plainsland—the Indians' home—opened to a white man's plow.

The final chapter was written when the army forced the fighting out of a series of sudden skirmishes and into an organized plan of relentless and grinding pursuits and midwinter campaigns with artillery, massed infantry, Gatling guns, the telegraph, the railroads and unlimited supplies.

Yet, throughout this bitter struggle, the warriors on both sides shared one thing in common—a kind of simple, stubborn, magnificent courage that still shines in the histories of their people.

GLOSSARY

Definitions of special words and terms which are not fully explained in text and pictures.

Adobe. Unburnt bricks of mud or clay dried in the sun.

Adjutant. Officer whose main duty is supervision, correspondence, orders, reports, requisitions and other paper work.

Accoutrements. Soldier's equipment other than clothes or weapons.

Commissary. Place of storage and distribution of food and rations.

Company. In the '60's and '70's, 80 to 100 men, noncommissioned officers and officers under command of captain.

Company barracks. Living quarters of enlisted men.

Detachment. Portion of troops from main body on special service.

Forage. Food for animals. 1863 regulation daily forage allowed 10 pounds of hay and 14 pounds of grain for each horse.

Guardhouse. Jail on a military post.

Hardtack. Hard, thin, square-shaped biscuit; sea biscuit.

Laundress. Woman paid for washing clothing of soldiers on military post, 4 laundresses allowed per company; often wives of noncommissioned officers.

Mule. Offspring of male ass and mare.

Near. Right side.

Noncommissioned officer. Sergeant or corporal; noncom; top kick.

"Nooning." Midday rest of troops on march.

Off. Left side.

"Old Army." Post-Civil War army from 1865 to about 1890.

Ordnance. Having to do with the care of artillery, small arms and ammunition.

Post fund. Money collected from tax on sutler, and savings on rations used to pay for bake-house; support of band, school and library.

Prairie belt. Type of nonregulation loop cartridge belt used in '60's and '70's; thimble belt.

Quartermaster. Having to do with providing quarters, clothing, transportation, forage, etc.

Rations. Daily allowance of food.

Regiment. In the '60's and '70's, 12 companies under command of colonel.

Sabre knot. Leather thong attached to hand guard and looped about wrist when sabre is in use.

"Shavetail." 2nd lieutenant; term thought to have come from army teamsters' habit of shaving tails of new, inexperienced mules.

FOR FURTHER READING ▬▬▬

A list of books and articles containing excellent general information about the history and people on the 1860-70 frontier would include the following:

Campbell, Walter Stanley (Stanley Vestal). *Warpath and Council Fire; the Plains Indians' Struggle for Survival in War and in Diplomacy.* New York: Random House, Inc., 1948.

Custer, Elizabeth. *Boots and Saddles.* New York: Harper and Brothers, 1885.

Custer, Elizabeth. *Following the Guidon.* New York: Harper and Brothers, 1890.

Custer, General G. A. *My Life on the Plains.* New York: Sheldon and Co., 1900.

Danker, D. F. (ed.). "The Journal of an Indian Fighter; the 1869 Diary of Major Frank J. North," *Nebraska History,* June, 1958.

Downey, Fairfax David. *Indian-Fighting Army.* New York: Charles Scribner's Sons, 1941.

Forsyth, George A. *The Story of the Soldier.* New York: Appleton-Century-Crofts, Inc., 1900.

Grinnell, George Bird. *Fighting Cheyennes.* Norman, Oklahoma: University of Oklahoma, 1956.

Herr, John K., and Edward S. Wallace. *Story of the U.S. Cavalry.* Boston: Little, Brown and Co., 1953.

Hull, Myra (ed.). "Soldiering on the High Plains: The Diary of Lewis Bryan Hull, 1864-1866," *Kansas Historical Quarterly,* February, 1938.

Mattison, Ray H. "The Army Post on the Northern Plains, 1865-1885," *Nebraska History,* March, 1954.

Ostrander, Alson Bowles. *Army Boy of the Sixties; a Story of the Plains.* Yonkers-on-the-Hudson: World Book Co., 1924.

Rickey, Don. "War in the West—The Indian Campaigns," *Custer Battlefield Historical and Museum Association,* Crown Agency, Montana, 1956.

Wellman, Paul Iselin. *Death on Horseback; Seventy Years of War for the American West.* New York: Garden City Publishing Co., 1950.

Welty, R. L. "The Army Post on the Frontier," *North Dakota Historical Quarterly,* April, 1928.

Welty, R. L. "The Frontier Army on the Missouri River, 1860-1870," *North Dakota Historical Quarterly,* January, 1928.

BIBLIOGRAPHY ▬▬▬

Much of the technical information appearing in this book came from the following sources:

Carter, Captain W. H. *Horses, Saddles and Bridles.* Leavenworth, Kan., 1895.

Hutchins. "Cavalry Campaign Outfit at the Little Big Horn," *Military Collector and Historian,* Winter, 1956.

Ordnance Manual for the Use of Officers of U.S. Army. New York: Lippincott and Co., 1862.

Outline Description of US Military Post and Stations in Year 1871, US Quartermaster Department.

Parson, John E. and John S. DuMont. *Firearms in the Custer Battle.* Harrisburg: Stackpole Co., 1954.

Regulations for Uniforms and Dress of Army of the US, July 1872, Adjutant General Office.

Childs. *Revised Regulations for the Army of U.S.,* 1863.

Safranek, V. F. *Complete Instructive Manual for the Bugle, Trumpet, Drum.* New York: Carl Fischer, Inc.

Uniforms of the US From 1774 to 1889, Quartermaster General. *U.S. Ordnance Department, Ordnance Memoranda No.'s 8, 13, 15, 18.*

ACKNOWLEDGMENTS

The author wishes to express his sincere gratitude to Miss Sally Johnson, Curator, National Park Service; Mr. R. B. Ringenback, Superintendent, Fort Laramie Historical Site; Messrs. Henry P. Roach and W. Ogden McCagg of the Company of Military Collectors and Historians; Mr. George Goldfine and the staff of the Sixth Army Reference Library, Presidio, San Francisco; P. M. Robinett, Brig. Gen. USA Ret.; to the Nebraska State Historical Society, the State Historical Society of North Dakota, the Kansas State Historical Society, and to all those whose kind consideration made this book possible.

The author is pleased to acknowledge the following sources for photographs and other material reproduced in this book.

"The Trooper" by Frederic Remington. Library of Congress.

Mounted Soldier in Great Coat. 41683A, U.S. National Museum, Washington, D.C.

Helmet for Mounted Officer. San Francisco Public Library.

Diagrams of suggested accoutrement changes; shoemaker bit; and drawing of regulation horse equipment, University of California Library, Berkeley, California.

Pawnee scouts. 1308-a-1, Bureau of American Ethnology, Smithsonian Institution.

Diagram of breech action and .50-calibre metallic cartridge. Bancroft Library, University of California.

Bugle music. Carl Fischer, Inc., New York.

Lyon's picket pin. University of California Library.

Cavalry Tactics title page. New York Public Library.

"Winter Attack on an Indian Village" by Frederic Remington. The Hogg Brothers Collection, The Museum of Fine Arts of Houston, Texas.

Gatling gun. San Francisco Public Library.

Sitting Bull photograph. 111-SC-83744, National Archives, Washington, D.C.